G000147373

mad for it

mad for it

The Wit & Wisdom of the Brothers Gallagher

Archivist: Paul Stokes

First published in Great Britain
2010 by Aurum Press Ltd
7 Greenland Street, London NW1 0ND
www.aurumpress.co.uk

A catalogue record for this book is
available from the British Library.

ISBN 978 1 84513 577 5

10 9 8 7 6 5 4 3 2 1
2014 2013 2012 2011 2010

Text design by Roger Hammond
Printed by MPG Books Ltd, Bodmin,
Cornwall

Contents

Introduction

Just two weeks before Christmas 1993 a review barely two-hundred words long appeared in weekly British music bible the *NME*. Recounting a gig at the Birmingham Institute that had taken place a week or so before, the article described the singer of the band in question as a 'slob of a frontman' before noting that 'If Oasis didn't exist, no one would want to invent them'. It was rare in the paper's early coverage of the Gallagher brothers' band in that it was negative, but as an incendiary it was vital: it triggered two of the greatest forces of nature music will ever know.

When Noel and Liam sat down in April of the following year to finally speak in the same publication, the singer was quick to make it clear that high on his list of priorities was the administering of 'a slap' to the writer of said review. With an air of confrontation hanging over the room, it wasn't long before the brothers' untamable comments turned on themselves, and then the world in general, as they chewed over riots on ferries and the idea of smacking each other in the face with musical instruments, before a row between the pair, remarkably about conkers, led to the interview being terminated in favour of a brotherly punch-up.

So entertaining, and genuinely funny,

was Noel and Liam's verbal joust, that the journalist refereeing the clash later edited down the recording and released it as a single entitled 'Wibling Rivalry'. It reached Number 52 in 1995 and remains the UK's highest-charting 'interview release'.

In an era where record companies routinely ship their new signings off for 'media training' to smooth any rough edges so they don't put the *X Factor* audience off their tea, we have to be thankful that whatever ticking off Oasis's management tried clearly didn't work. Indeed, far from being a youthful indiscretion, the outburst represented the opening salvo in a lifetime of outspoken, uncompromising and ultimately hilarious utterances from British rock 'n' roll's most notorious fraternity.

If the pair had never recorded *Definitely Maybe*, the bickering brothers from

mad for it

Burnage would probably still have become infamous in Manchester, but instead, as the driving forces behind Oasis, the world has been privy, whether it liked it or not, to the Gallagher brothers' pronouncements. And, let's face it, they've been hard to ignore. From taking indie music out of scuzzy little clubs and on to the national news when they went head-to-head with Blur at the height of Britpop, to becoming one of the few British bands of modern times to make Wembley Stadium a home-from-home, Oasis have loomed large over British culture for nearly two decades. With a lot of young musicians now confessing that it was Noel and Liam who first made them want to be in a band, even their acrimonious break-up in 2009 hasn't stopped the pair's words from resonating.

Whether critiquing their own band,

casting brutal judgment on their rivals, or
making sense of everything from our reality-
TV obsessed modern culture, the fortunes
of Manchester City Football Club to high
politics (even joking about drug taking with
a serving Prime Minister at Ten Downing
Street), Noel and Liam Gallagher are not the
kind of musicians who shrug their shoulders
and claim to 'make music for themselves'.
Rather, they are more than happy to let the
world know what they think – and more
often than not that has included their full
and frank verdicts on each other. Forget
flogging records or basking in their own
glory, Oasis's encounters with the media
have generally seen the brothers use
interviews and TV shows as a forum for
taking potshots at each other. In fact, even
though the brothers were no longer on
speaking terms when Oasis split up

(though they had plenty to say *about* each other), there has been no let up in the verbal volleys.

Of course, over-opinionated rock stars are nothing new, but what stops the Gallaghers being the pub bores of the music world is the fact that no matter whether you agree with what they say or not, you want to hear them say it. Noel could easily have traded being one of the greatest songwriters of his generation for being one of its greatest stand-ups; while tucked away within Liam's 'mad fer it' stance are some almost Zen-like insights.

Today, having incurred the wrath of everyone from Archbishops, superstar rappers and various police forces the world over, it's clear the brothers' words and opinions know no limits.

As Kasabian's Tom Meighan – who

toured with Oasis and had the privilege of observing the Gallagher brothers close up – has noted, for all their bluster, a wealth of wit *and* wisdom informs Noel and Liam's pronouncements.

'Oasis kind of pull the book open and read to you, they tell you the story while you're in bed listening – know what I mean?' he said of the insights inherent within the Gallagher outlook. 'They're great men, they just believe. They've been there and done it.'

And what they've done, more than anything else, is talk about it …

The Early Days

Despite the Gallagher brothers being synonymous with Oasis, neither Noel nor Liam was in the band when it originally started under the name Rain in Manchester in 1991. In fact, despite Noel's impending dominance of the group, it was his younger sibling who was first to sign up, after guitarist Paul 'Bonehead' Arthurs auditioned him to join bassist Paul 'Guigsy' McGuigan and curly-haired drummer Tony McCarroll. However, Liam wasn't slow to begin the Gallagher takeover, suggesting the name Oasis, inspired by a leisure centre in Swindon with the same moniker. Not that Noel was marking time; the elder Gallagher was touring as a roadie with fellow Mancunians Inspiral Carpets, quietly working on the songs that he would present to Oasis when he signed up. In a strange twist of fate, Alan McGee, head of

Creation Records, had deliberately avoided the band in the winter of 1992 when visiting Manchester, after being put off by the Union Jack on their drumkit. A year later though they had his full attention, storming the stage at Glasgow's King Tut's Wah Wah Hut to play for him. Needless to say, a record contract was offered there and then.

. . .

Oasis's first influences

'I can't explain but when I saw the Stone Roses on stage it did something to me. They were real people doing it from the heart and just treated everything about themselves dead special, which is right.'
Liam 1994

. . .

'*Nevermind The Bollocks* is the record that changed my life ... My mum fucking hated it. Very Catholic, so she didn't approve of tracks like 'Bodies'. It had to be really good if she didn't like it. She even used to hide the record from me so I bought it on tape and hid it in my pocket.'

Noel 1995

. . .

'I just wanted to be in a band and I wanted to tour the fucking world and I wanted to shag all the fucking birds and that was the end of it. I wanted to drink and get fucking pissed and off my tits and as high as I could possibly get. And be paid for it.'
Liam 2004

. . .

'Although we all hung around the same area together, and we'd known each other virtually all our lives we weren't a gang. Gangs don't make music, gangs sell drugs and steal cars, you know what I mean.'
Noel 2007

. . .

On their early burglary years

'I'd nick lawn mowers and sell 'em for weed.'
Liam 2002

. . .

'What people fail to understand
is that we never started this
band as a career move. We did
it because we were bored
shitless on the dole .'
Noel 2001

. . .

'When everyone else was necking Es and going
out dancing to fucking Dalek music in The
Haçienda, I was trying to make a band.'
Liam 2004

. . .

On being a roadie

'I look back on those days as some of the best of my life. No photographs, no interviews. Just get up in the morning, make sure the gear works, do the gig and then fucking party.'

Noel 2008

. . .

On their first few gigs

'We were actually trying to convince people we were great, but after the first few gigs in Manchester no one would put us on because we had this reputation for being ... not lads, just difficult. We had a fight with the headlining band one night 'cause they pulled the plug on us in the last song ... it got us a bit of a reputation.'

Noel 1994

. . .

'We were crazy, we should have died.
But I don't believe in death.'
Liam 1997

. . .

'I was always open to other people writing in this
band, but no cunt ever did.'
Noel 2000

. . .

'The best bit about the early days was when our
kid got chinned. That geezer jumped onstage and
lamped him in the eye.'
Liam 1997

. . .

'I remember my mum sitting me down one night
and saying, "What is going to become of you?"
And I didn't have an answer. But she never once
told me to get a proper job or settle down and get
married. She used to say, "You better not let me
down", and I have not.'
Noel 1996

. . .

On the early nineties

'At the time [Oasis emerged] it was just Phil Collins and all these boring people and boring bands playing gigs ... You don't look like rock stars, you look like dicks in tights, like something off a pantomime. It was time for some real lads to get up there and take charge.'

Liam 2002

. . .

On the night Oasis played for Alan McGee in Glasgow

'We didn't threaten to burn the club down. We just pointed out to the owner of the club that if he didn't let us play, there were fifteen of us and three of them. So he did a quick mathematical assumption that it was probably in his best interests to let us play.'

Noel 2004

. . .

On youthful ambition

'I used to say we were going to be the biggest band in Britain and I think Liam and McGee just went along with it, but I honestly believed we were going to be as big as The Beatles, I really did. I believed we were going to be massive.'

Noel 2007

. . .

'I think we'll be the most important band in the fucking world. If time is on our side, and there's not so much bad shit, and no one dies, we'll be the new Beatles.'

Liam 1994

. . .

'Any advice for young
musicians?
Always wear a condom.'

Liam 1996

. . .

On Manchester

'That city's done us no favours, man.'
Noel 1994

. . .

**However, whatever their feelings on
their home town, you can take the boys
out of the city, but you can't take the
city out of the boys**

'We've got a little Mancunian
corner of north London. You'll
have noticed, it's the area with
no hubcaps on the cars.'
Noel 1997

Liam on Noel

Noel Gallagher was born on 29 May 1967, in Manchester, the second son to Tommy and Peggy Gallagher. Noel was brought up in the city's Burnage neighbourhood and, after an early career of truancy, police bother and a spot of hooliganism, the future songwriter was expelled from school aged fifteen. Following stints on building sites, on the dole and roadieing for Manchester baggy band Inspiral Carpets, Noel returned to join – well, take over – younger brother Liam's band Oasis. So, who better to give his verdict on the man they call 'The Chief'? The boy who shared bunk beds with him right back at the start: Liam.

. . .

On brotherly love

'I'm Jack, our kid's Vera.'
Liam 2002

. . .

'I win nearly all of our fights. He's caused me a bit of harm, but that's about it. Big brothers are supposed to be harder but he's chilled out and I'm not. He's seen a lot of things I haven't. I'm more of a nutter, I've got more aggression. We don't fight as much as we used to. We chatted about it months ago and decided to cool down a bit.'
Liam 1995

. . .

'We're not mates. We just don't feel like it. We get on better when we don't see each other and don't speak to each other.'
Liam 2000

. . .

'Well I hate this bastard and that's what it's about. That's why we'll be the best band in the world: 'cause I fucking hate that twat there and I hope there's a time where I can smash the fuck out of him with a fucking Rickenbacker. Right on his nose. Then he can do the same to me.'

Liam 1994

. . .

'Who knows, man, maybe he needs to go and do his solo record … it would sound very civilised I reckon. It's an awful thing, but maybe it's a good thing for him.'

Liam 2009

. . .

mad for it

'If we weren't in a band, we'd be having rows in the house. If we had a greengrocers, Gallagher's Greengrocers, we'd argue over which way to set out the apples or pears.'
Liam 1995

. . .

On singing Noel's words

'I'm the singer and the only personal lyrics of his I'm singing is, "I've got a 12-inch cock, d'ya want some?" I don't mind singing that.'
Liam 2002

. . .

'I tell you, when I read that Oasis is Noel's band that fucking sent me ... It's no one's band. It's all of us. Take one away and there's nowt left.'
Liam 1994

. . .

**Indeed 'ownership' of Oasis has
always been something of a sore point
between the pair, as this 1998
exchange proved ...**

Noel: 'It's not my band.'

Liam: 'Whose band is it?'

Noel: 'It's your band.'

Liam: 'Hang on a minute ... It's not my band
now that we're shit and nobody likes
us!'

Noel: 'It's your band.'

Liam: 'It was my band when we were popular.
You sneaky bastard!'

. . .

**Not that Liam hasn't pulled one over
'The Chief' from time to time, most
impressively onstage during their 1996
Knebworth House gigs**

. . .

Noel: 'This is history, right here, right now, this is
history!'

Liam: 'No it fucking isn't, you daft twat, it's
Knebworth.'

. . .

And then, onstage at the Brit Awards Liam clearly forgot who Noel was when receiving an award for *(What's The Story) Morning Glory?*

'Listen kids, I wanna thank Bonehead, Guigs, Alan White and the best fucking fans in the world.'
Liam 2010

. . .

'Who is the most overrated person of all time? Has to be Noel Gallagher.'
Liam 2010

. . .

'It takes a lot more than blood to be my brother.'
Liam 2009

Noel on Liam

Born on 21 September 1972 and christened William John Paul Gallagher, Liam Gallagher hasn't done badly for a young troublemaker who, according to his older brothers, showed no interest in music until his late teens. Not only was he the first Gallagher in Oasis, Liam has since gone on to set himself up as a would-be fashion designer with his label, Pretty Green. He's also contemplating breaking into the film business. So what makes this self-confessed 'lad' tick? Having been forced to share a bedroom with him at their family home, as well as plenty of studios and tour buses since, here's Noel's assessment of 'What's'izname'.

'Liam's the Tasmanian Devil ... I'm Mr Burns off
The Simpsons.'
Noel 2000

. . .

'Liam has got more stupid.
When he was at school he was
quite normal. Now he's
definitely mad. He's not mad
like some people in bands are
mad. He's madder than mad ...
He's just mad.'

Noel 1995

. . .

To Liam in 1994 after the band were deported from Holland after causing trouble on a cross-channel ferry

Noel: 'If you're proud of getting thrown off ferries why don't you go and support West Ham and get the fuck out of my band and go and be a football hooligan. We're musicians, right.'

Liam: 'You're only gutted because you were in bed, reading your fucking books …'

.   .   .

'I never get a phone call off Liam unless it's a problem.'
Noel 1998

.   .   .

'I like to think I keep it real. Liam keeps it surreal, and somewhere between the two we get on all right.'
Noel 2007

.   .   .

'Liam doesn't like me. He confuses love with hate. "I love you." No, Liam, I think you'll find you fucking hate me.'
Noel 2006

. . .

On one of Liam's many absences

'He's gone to the zoo. The monkeys are bringing their kids to go and have a look at him.'
Noel 2002

. . .

'Liam, of course, who is like a woman who's on a fucking permanent menstrual cycle all the time about everything, he's either way up in the clouds or way down in the gutter.'
Noel 2005

. . .

'Liam used to really annoy me, but now I think he is a comic genius.'
Noel 2001

. . .

On Liam's inability to hold his tongue

'It's typical of Liam. Seven in the morning on Oxford Street, two policemen ask him what he's up to and instead of being polite he says, "What's it got to do with you, cuntybollocks?"'
Noel 1997

. . .

'He's rude, arrogant, intimidating and lazy. He's the angriest man you'll ever meet. He's like a man with a fork in a world of soup.'
Noel 2009

. . .

'I read these interviews with him and I don't know who the guy is who's in these interviews, he seems really cool, because the guy I've been in a band with for the last eighteen years is a fucking knobhead.'
Noel 2008

. . .

mad for it

On Liam imitating John Lennon

'He was talking in a Scouse accent for three days. He told me I should refer to him as John and I was like, "I just prefer 'cunt', man."'
Noel 2005

. . .

Not that Noel is entirely down on his younger brother, occasionally he even admits Liam might be the cooler Gallagher...

'Liam is the life and soul of the party. I probably always stand in the kitchen.'
Noel 2001

. . .

'The thing about Liam and his hairdos is when he gets a new one you think "That looks absolutely rubbish" then six weeks later everyone on Oxford Street has got one.'
Noel 2007

. . .

After seeing footage of Liam dancing enthusiastically backstage in their tour documentary *Lord Don't Slow Me Down*

'Fucking mental. I tell you what, I'm going to keep my eye on those rooms he goes in next time we go on tour. What are you doing on stage standing there with your hands behind your back? That's rubbish now I've seen the golden drifter in the room!'

Noel 2007

. . .

However, not everything works out well between the pair onstage, as this exchange in 2000, after Liam forgot the words to 'Stand By Me' in Tokyo, shows ...

Noel: 'If you'd turn up at the rehearsals you'd know the words. Perhaps if we had the speakers plugged into the nearest pub we'd be alright.'

Liam: 'Has anyone got any biscuits?'

. . .

mad for it

Or there's always Wembley ...

'The second night [in 2000] was quite
monumental, because Liam had been out with a
Spice Girl the night before – a Spice Girl – and he
didn't bother going to bed. It was the first comedy
performance at the old Wembley.'
Noel 2008

. . .

'I feel sorry for our kid sometimes. I get all this
going on inside my head and I can write it all down
and get off on that. But he can't, so his release is
to get off his head.'
Noel 1994

. . .

That said, Liam's pretty sure
of things ...

'Who am I? What do you mean,
"Who am I?"
I'm the fucking man!'
Liam 2009

The Gallaghers
on Oasis

If your surname isn't Gallagher, being in Oasis is rather like being a member of the most exclusive, yet eccentric, members' club in the world. If you're in you have a pass to travel the globe, reach the pinnacle of rock 'n' roll and bask in luxury. However, one wrong word to the membership committee (Noel 'n' Liam) and you can be out without any explanation; particularly if you're a drummer. From the founding line up (with Tony McCarroll, Bonehead and Paul 'Guigsy' McGuigan) to Gem Archer and Andy Bell, who were still onboard when the band split in 2009, Noel and Liam have never been shy in voicing their opinions about their fellow band members, their output or even their fans' devotion, with their albums and the record-buying public sometimes getting as short a shrift as the last drummer they've sacked. Put simply: these Gallagher boys are very hard to please indeed.

. . .

'You can't predict anything with my band, anything can happen. I can actually envision a day you'll be over the Indian Ocean and an air stewardess will come back and say, "Mr Gallagher? Your brother has fallen out of the plane." I'd be like, "Where's he landed? Is it shark invested? Great!"'
Noel 2005

. . .

'We're not fucking wizards. We're four blokes from Manchester who happen to be in the best band in the world.'
Liam 2002

. . .

'We've not got respect for any crowd, not even our own ... I look at it this way: £32.50 is nowhere near enough money to come and see me play guitar. It should be £32.50 for each member of the band, it's that fucking good!'
Noel 2005

. . .

Not that they want to upset all their fans ...

'The last time we were there [New York], there was loads of the fucking Mob turning up because apparently they're big Oasis fans. So, there's this big block of seats and it's all guys with suits and sunglasses ... I was looking out for Tony Soprano down the front.'
Noel 2001

. . .

mad for it

On their albums

Definitely Maybe
'Look. I was a superhero in the '90s. I said so at the time. McCartney, Weller, Townshend, Richards, my first album's better than all their first albums. Even they'd admit that.'
Noel 2006

. . .

(What's The Story) Morning Glory?
'I personally think *Definitely Maybe* is a far better album [than *(What's The Story) Morning Glory?*] and can't understand why in this country in particular people who went and bought *Morning Glory* didn't buy *Definitely Maybe*. I'd just like to say, "Where do you get off on that?" ... "What's that all about, do you just do it to piss me off?" I can think about that for hours. People are fucking weird.'
Noel 2002

. . .

On learning Berwick Street, London, bears a plaque because it's on the cover of the same album

'Do you think people do the thing, walking down the street like they do at Abbey Road? That would be fucking great wouldn't it? I wouldn't mind but it's such a fucking shit cover. It must be one of the most uninspired artworks for one of the biggest albums of all time. I'd like to think Japanese people do walk down that street in rush hour dodging black cabs.'
Noel 2007

. . .

Be Here Now
'People can bitch about it for the rest of their lives, fucking sell it! You can get four or five quid for it, I imagine. Come round to my house and I'll sign it for you, you'd probably get a tenner then.'
Noel 2002

. . .

Standing On The Shoulder Of Giants
'I won't lie. Half the stuff on Standing On The Shoulder Of Giants doesn't even stand up to the old stuff. Compared to the first album. If people want it, great, go and buy it. It's under O, next to the fucking Osmonds.'
Noel 2002

. . .

Heathen Chemistry

'It's exactly what you'd expect from us and that's not to sound narrow minded. A lot of bands these days go out of their way not to sound like themselves. If anything we've gone the other route. We're desperately trying to sound like Oasis.'
Noel 2001

. . .

Don't Believe The Truth

'Someone said to me all my songs sound like b-sides from 1994, they're that good. I said thanks very much, I take that as a compliment because the b-sides I wrote between '94 and '95 should have been on *Be Here Now* but weren't. That would be an insult to some people, but not to me.'
Noel 2005

. . .

Dig Our Your Soul
'It's not blown me away.'
Liam 2009

. . .

On their bandmates

'There's no point in interviewing them, they've got fuck all to say for themselves anyway.'
Noel 1994 [*referring to everyone in Oasis bar Liam*]

. . .

On the entry criteria for potential new band members

'They've got to be a lot taller than me, have nice taste in shoes and a decent haircut and not be Man U fans. If you can do that, you're sorted.'
Liam 1999

. . .

On sacking their first drummer Tony McCarroll

'He was being lazy. He was being rude to the customers.'
Liam 1995

. . .

'What would I say if I bumped into Tony McCarroll on the street? Do you want to borrow a fiver?'
Liam 2000

. . .

On sacking second drummer Alan White

'We've only ever had four band meetings in twelve years, so once they're called they're pretty fucking serious … Turns out he's hanging out with his bird in Spain. Once the words "bird" and "Spain" are mentioned together it's like, "OK, Oasis vs girlfriend."'
Noel 2005

. . .

Next came Ringo Starr's son on the sticks …

'When you say a sex turkey, do you mean Zak Starkey?'
Noel 2009 [speaking to a foreign interviewer]

. . .

Hopefully by now prospective Oasis drummers had got the message

'Do we have any rituals before going onstage? There's always the new drummer. "Enjoy yourself, this is probably your last gig". We've a strange relationship in the band; it'd freak most people out.'
Noel 2008

. . .

Not that it's just drummers who got the heave-ho. Rhythm guitarist Paul 'Bonehead' Arthurs was the next founder member to go ...

'It's hardly Paul McCartney leaving the The Beatles. It happens, things happen.'
Noel 1999

. . .

Followed by bassist Guigsy ...

'I don't want to slag Guigsy and Bonehead off, but them leaving and Gem and Andy coming in has been the saving of Oasis.'
Noel 2001

. . .

However, they seemed to be a bit softer on the new boys

'We went for a curry with Gem and asked him to join the band. That was it. It wasn't like a fucking job interview.'
Liam 2001

. . .

'Andy's "Stones, Stones, Stones" all the time and Liam's "Beatles, Beatles, Beatles". There was like a fucking Mexican stand off one night in a bar. After we got past that we knew it was going to be fine.'
Noel 2001

. . .

'I can't tell anybody what to do in the band now it's this new democracy. There's no referee and it looks like it's just going to drift. It'll end up in an almighty fight.'
Noel 2001

The Gallaghers vs The World

Surveying his Britpop rivals as Oasis first emerged in 1994, Noel Gallagher was taken aback by what the likes of Suede and Blur felt was appropriate material for song lyrics. 'We're not preaching about ye olde England or how it was in the '60s,' he declared. 'We're not preaching about our sexuality, we're not telling people how to act. You want to write about shagging and taking drugs and being in a band. You don't want to write about going down the supermarket or anything like that – I know it's terrible so I'm not going to write about it.'

Yet while an Oasis song might not tell you much about the state of the nation, Liam and Noel have not been as reticent about the wider world – let's not forget Noel's cocktail party with Tony Blair at Number Ten in 1997 – in real life. In fact if you look at the Gallaghers's views on politics, sport, the environment and even getting a pint of Guinness in Afghanistan, it's obvious why they don't write about the world in their songs: they'd never fit it all in ...

. . .

On arts and literature

'My favourite book is *The Lion, The Witch and The Wardrobe.* I like it. I like that thing of just going into a wardrobe.'
Liam 1997

. . .

On the global economic crisis

'I was asked to explain what I thought had gone
wrong with the global economy … we managed to
trace back the actual moment the storm clouds
started to gather to when Franz Ferdinand won the
Mercury Muzak Prize. Think about it.'
Noel 2009

. . .

'I think the world is at a critical point. Like an
elastic band, where it's either going to snap or
people are going to come to their senses.'
Noel 2008

. . .

On the intricacies of politics

'Doesn't matter who you fucking vote for. It'll still
be shit unless you join a band.'
Liam 2010

. . .

'Vote Labour. If you don't and the Tories get in,
Phil Collins is threatening to come back from
Switzerland and live here – and none of us want
that.'
Noel 2005

. . .

mad for it

On drugs culture

'I've got a cover of the *Daily Mirror* that says, "98 per cent back Noel on drugs", which is a great headline. One for the grandkids, innit?'
Noel 1997

. . .

On visiting Ten Downing Street to meet Tony Blair in 1997

'We'd watched the election all through the night and I asked Tony Blair how he managed to stay up all night. He leaned towards me and said, "Probably not by the same means you did!"'
Noel 2002

. . .

'It looks like a shit house, so why go there?'
Liam 2002

. . .

'I'm glad I did it to have a look, but in terms of New Labour, I recognise now that we were conned. We thought Blair was John F. Kennedy, when in fact he was John Major with a better PR team.'
Noel 2001

. . .

'Would I accept an MBE? Yeah, I would because you could probably flog it. I'd rather he offered me a place in the fucking cabinet. Minister for rock! They've got a minister for sport, all that bollocks, running around in shorts and that. Fuck that nonsense!'
Noel 1995

. . .

On religion

'About bringing the mountain to Mohammed – are we still allowed to say that? I recall an incident with a teddy bear recently.'
Noel 2009

. . .

On globalisation

'Watched the match … at an Irish bar! They're everywhere. I bet there's one in Kabul.'
Noel 2009

. . .

On the environment

'You can't blame rock stars for global warming when the Chinese, the Indians and the Americans have been pumping out shit into the atmosphere for the last hundred years.'
Noel 2008

. . .

On the East-West divide

'Yorkshire people are not a race. You are just a collective of idiots.'
Noel 2008

. . .

Explaining why he trashed a room at London's Columbia Hotel

'There was a bug in my room and I thought, "You can fuck off, this is my room".'
Liam 1994

. . .

On charity concert Live8

'Correct me if I am wrong, but are they hoping that
one of these guys from the G8 is going to see
Annie Lennox singing 'Sweet Dreams' and think,
"Fuck me, she might have a point there!"?'
Noel 2005

. . .

Summing up the more litigious nature
of modern society

'I'm up for lamping people, but not these days.
You can lamp 'em when you've got no money, but
when you've got loads of money you can't lamp
because they sue you.'
Liam 1997

. . .

On the threat of global pandemics

'Got myself a pig flu mask and I must say, I quite
like it. Makes me feel a little like a James Bond
baddy and look like an evil genius. No wonder
Michael Jackson wears them all the time.'
Noel 2009

. . .

On the press

'I don't see how the tabloids could get any worse for me unless they claimed I'd had anal sex with an alien. "Liam Gallagher was caught last night bending an alien across a pool table and poking his bottom." What more can they say about me?'

Liam 1997

. . .

On downloading music

'I think it's fucking scandalous. They should get their hands in their pockets and get down the shops like the rest of us.'

Liam 2000

. . .

'So what happens now then? Do I actually have to buy a bastard computer to buy music? Where is it going to end? I may have to move to Japan!'

Noel 2009

. . .

'I think the current prices [for albums] are OK, what is it, £7.99 online? That's enough to keep my swimming pool full of mineral water.'
Noel 2008

. . .

On television

'I just want to know what were those fuckers hoping to achieve out of this [*Pop Idol*]? What was that twat Dr Fox, and those other cunts, doing? Did they really think they'd find the new Elvis? They've made a mockery of singing, of selling a million records. Will Young is in *The Guinness Book of Records* for fuck's sale! But so what? So is a bloke who jumps off the Eiffel Tower and lands in a fucking tea cup. Did he write 'Strawberry Fields Forever'? No. So fuck off.'
Noel 2002

. . .

On football crowds

'Mexican waves? I never got involved in all that, I don't even like it at gigs or anything like that, it shows that nothing is going on on the pitch. At the snooker, I don't mind.'
Noel 2010

. . .

On the royal family

'They are always going to be here, just like lampposts.'
Liam 2000

. . .

On everyday life

'I stand in the queue at Waitrose. More rock stars should do that. Forget therapy, go to the supermarket and interact. The staff in my local Waitrose are really blasé about me now. They'll be like, "Him? Oh, he's in here all the fucking time. And between me and you, he doesn't eat very well".'
Noel 2006

The Gallaghers on The Music

With outside interests including everything from sport punditry (Noel) and a fashion label (Liam), not to mention the fact that interviews with them seem to cover every subject under the sun, it's possible to overlook that the Gallagher brothers' 'trade' is actually music. However, led by Noel, the pair have been responsible for some of the biggest anthems ever produced, not to mention million-selling albums and global mega-gigs. They can even be heard talking about it, on occasion …

. . .

On the creative art of song writing

'There's ... meaning in the songs. I don't
know what they mean, but there's still meaning
there. They mean things, but I just don't
exactly know what.'

Liam 1996

. . .

'I met this girl the other night and I felt sorry for
her, because she came up to me and said
(quietly), "I've got 'Supersonic' and I'm really
into your lyrics and I've been through a lot as
well." And I went, "What do you mean?
'Supersonic' is about some fucking nine-stone
geezer who got Charlied off his nut one night ...
it's not about anything!"'

Noel 1994

. . .

'Noel writes the songs, but we've all got ears. Noel needs to be told and I tell him. That's how half our rucks start...'
Liam 1995

. . .

On quality control

'I don't believe people can go into a studio and record b-sides. It's either a good song or a bad song, and I never intend to write a bad song!'
Noel 1998

. . .

One such b-side 'Acquiesce' even saw the Gallaghers dueting in 1996

'It [the title] was good because it confused Liam. "What's a fucking acquiesce?" "It's a new car by Volkswagen. Fucking great, you wanna get yourself one".'
Noel 1998

. . .

'If Liam doesn't like it, he doesn't sing it. It's as simple as that. Or if there's something more important to do going on, like a pub crawl, then he won't do it. Bless him.

Lager before music.'

Noel 1998

. . .

'What the fuck do producers do anyway? Sit there, drink coffee and tell you how shit you are.'

Liam 2003

. . .

A digression on progression from 1994

Liam: 'You can progress sideways or backwards. I'm right though, tell me I'm not!'

Noel: 'Progression is going forwards. Going backwards is regression. Going sideways is just gression.'

. . .

On maintaining a healthy sense of self-belief

'There's one [song] called 'Songbird' which is better than anything on *Revolver*.'
Liam 2001

. . .

'Liam says he's written some songs that are better than the ones on The Beatles' *Revolver*. It's bullshit. Nobody is capable of writing anything better than the songs on *Revolver* ...
He's not as good as John Lennon. He's not even as good as Jack Lemmon, God bless him ... He's not in John Lennon's class. Only I am capable of that.'
Noel 2000

. . .

'*Be Here Now* has shockingly bad lyrics, but I will
say in my own demonic, drug-induced state I
wrote an album in fourteen days – count them –
that sold seven-and-a-half-million copies. If I'd
actually tried at that point in my life I'd have
been fucking God.'
Noel 2001

. . .

'No one writes about getting high any more.
They're writing about their grandparents.'
Noel 2001

. . .

'Liam can only sing one way.
You put the mic there, you put
the beers there, the fags there,
and you just wind him up and
wind him up until he gets that
irate and he screams his
bollocks off.'
Noel 1998

. . .

'I don't sit down and go, "I'm gonna make music that's gonna be sung by the gods of fucking Uranus for the next 5,000 aeons." What can I say to you? I fucking play guitar in a fucking rock 'n' roll band. You can take it or leave it.'
Noel 2002

. . .

Once the songs are written and the album is recorded, the Gallaghers hit the road, which, with missed gigs, members storming out and more, usually provide its fair share of fireworks

'If I can't feel the wind from the amps making my trousers flap, then I'd rather go fucking shopping.'
Noel 2002

. . .

'I don't go on the road to make money – it just so happens we do – I go on the road to have a laugh and play my rock 'n' roll and that's the fucking end of it, and if anyone tries to tell me any different they're off their fucking tits.'
Liam 2001

. . .

'I don't want people watching me and thinking, "I could do that". I want them thinking they could never do that.'
Noel 1995

. . .

'There's no point blitzing America. Whatever is meant to happen in this walk of life, man, will happen. Whatever will be, will be. Why be in a band if we're all going to end up in the cuckoo farm?'

Liam 1996

.   .   .

'It's always the same [touring the US]. It starts off great and then somewhere, usually America, I don't know why ... probably the sight of cactus plants or something like that ... it freaks Liam out. Then he oversteps the mark a little bit and ... it degenerates from there.'

Noel 2005

.   .   .

'You spend seven months on the road in a complete fucking rock 'n' roll bubble, being treated like a child, so you act like a child. Then you come back expecting to pick up where you left off and find out life goes on without you ... Now I'm living in a hotel with a bar that's open all night ... I haven't passed anything solid out of my arse for two months.'

Noel 2000

.   .   .

Not that the Gallaghers made it to every gig

Liam: 'We're not U2, INXS or Simple Minds! Those cunts are so in it for the money they'll carry on whatever. With me, if I've got something better to do, something more important, I'm fucking doing it. If you want your money back I'll personally give it back to you.'

Noel: 'Can I just say, for legal reasons, there will be no refunds.'

2002

. . .

There have been some novel excuses for cancelled shows over the years, the best being ...

'We had a few months off after Liam got relieved of his teeth in Germany.'
Noel 2005

. . .

Although the band do occasionally behave themselves on the road

'Some bands have whores and cocaine in the dressing room. What do we have? Board games! Board games are where it's at!'
Noel 2007

. . .

During their time together, the Gallaghers headlined many of the world's greatest festivals

'I could put my professional hat on and I could say that it's really important to come and play for these people for the social aspect of Rock In Rio. Or I could be honest and say it's really fucking cold in England and it's really warm here.'
Noel 2002

. . .

On Glastonbury

'Glasto is great to be at, but it's not great for people like us to play at. You're on at 11.00, and the people you're with are absolutely battered. Your girlfriend stops making sense.'
Noel 2008

. . .

mad for it

But it's their gigs at Knebworth House in Hertfordshire in 1996 – at the time the largest free-standing concert organised by a band in the UK – that are widely accepted as their biggest live achievement

'I think if we'd have sat down and calculated that we were going to make history, I would have certainly worn a better outfit, maybe gone to bed a bit earlier and tried to keep Liam off the sauce.'
Noel 2002

. . .

'I'm very proud of that. What do I remember about it? Nothing.'
Liam 2002

The Gallaghers
on Other Bands

'I want to stop slagging other bands off because I've met most of them and they're really nice people,' declared Noel Gallagher in 1995, 'but I have to be honest and say that they're not very good.' And fortunately for us neither Gallagher senior nor his brother has kept their council when it's come to their rivals, their contemporaries and even their heroes. Often as insightful as, and certainly more cutting than most music critics, the Gallaghers have provided an invaluable commentary to popular culture. In one case, a rivalry with a certain band called Blur, Noel and Liam's views contributed one of the defining battles of Britpop …

.   .   .

'Everything is shit – in my world. I'm not gonna spend time watchin' some stupid little band that a) don't look good, that b) haven't got any tunes, and c) they want a career out of music. I'm not in it for a career. I'm here to touch people.'
Liam 2010

. . .

That means Oasis's contemporaries ...

'Scissor Sisters? It's just music for hairdressers isn't it? My daughter's five and she fucking loves them. Say no more.'
Noel 2005

. . .

On Kurt Cobain

'Don't talk to me about Nirvana. He was a sad man who couldn't handle the fame.'
Liam 1994

. . .

On Pete Doherty

'I'm not into smackheads; smackheads need slaps.'
Liam 2005

.   .   .

'I'll tell you what, he needs to wash his hands more.'
Noel 2005

.   .   .

On Radiohead

'Radiohead are a band of Morris dancers.'
Liam 2002

.   .   .

On Keane

'Traditionally speaking, throughout the history of rock 'n' roll, the three biggest twats in any band are always the singer, the keyboard [player] and the drummer. You can't argue with that!'
Noel 2005

.   .   .

On Kasabian's Sergio Pizzorno

'I like him 'cause of other reasons. [But] He's been told about the pointy shoes, been told, man.'
Liam 2009

. . .

On Arctic Monkeys

'When I first met Arctic Monkeys they came in our dressing room and they were a right cool bunch of kids. Then Alex said he got a guitar because of Oasis … he was nine when *Definitely Maybe* came out. That bent my head.'
Noel 2007

. . .

On Florence + the Machine

'I'm not having anyone with ginger hair making music. I can't go down that road. I'm sure she's a nice girl but she sounds like someone has stood on her fucking foot.'
Liam 2010

. . .

On The White Stripes

'Jack White has just done a song for Coca-Cola.
End of. He ceases to be in the club. And he looks
like Zorro on doughnuts. He's supposed to be the
poster boy for the alternative way of thinking ... I'm
not having that, that's fucking wrong. Particularly
Coca-Cola, it's like doing a fucking gig for
McDonald's.'
Noel 2005

. . .

'Our kid's big thing at the moment is that
The Strokes are crap "because their singer's
called Julian".'
Noel 2001

. . .

On Amy Winehouse

'She's a destitute horse.'
Noel 2008

. . .

Worse still, though, you could be a pop star ...

'For some reason I watched MTV's European Top Ten. Fuck me, it was painful. Leona Lewis doing Snow Patrol? Ouch! Kings of Leon doing U2? Ouch! The Killers doing fancy dress? Ouch! Lady Gaga? It made my teeth hurt.'
Noel 2009

. . .

On Robbie Williams

'A lot of people want to have sex with me, and he's at the fucking back of the list.'
Liam 2001

. . .

On celebrities 'writing' their memoirs

'Why is Posh Beckham writing a fucking book of her memoirs? She can't even chew chewing gum and walk in a fucking straight line at the same time, let alone write a book.'
Noel 2001

. . .

On novelty records

'I remember when there were good novelty records and nobody gave a fuck. Now Bob The Builder's number one and Mel C is phoning him up wanting to do a duet! A fucking builder and a joiner! All you need is Ronan Keating and you've got a builder, a joiner and a fucking plasterer! They'd be better off starting their own firm …'
Noel 2001

. . .

On Robbie again

'Robbie's still officially on strike isn't he? From being brilliant.'
Noel 2008

. . .

And even music 'legends' are in the firing line ...

On U2

'Play 'One', shut the fuck up about Africa.'
Noel 2007

. . .

On Elvis Presley

'My fascination with Elvis? Just wiping his arse with gooses' necks does it for me.'
Liam 2000

. . .

After receiving an award from INXS's, Michael Hutchence

'Has-beens should be presenting fucking awards to gonna-bes.'
Noel 1996

. . .

On rock's elder statesmen

'We've just done a cover of The Stones' 'Street Fighting Man' just to piss them off ... I'm going to shoot my mouth off here – all these snakes coming out of the closets, all these old farts, I'll offer them out right here. If they want to fight, be at Primrose Hill, Saturday morning, 12 o'clock. I will beat the fucking living daylights out of them, that goes for George [Harrison], Jagger, Richards and any other cunts that give a shit ... they're jealous and senile and not getting enough fucking meat pies.'
Liam 1997

. . .

'If I'd have been born at the same time as John Lennon, I'd have been up there. Well, I'd definitely have been better than Gerry and the fucking Pacemakers, I know that.'
Noel 1996

. . .

'John Lennon would probably hate us, then again who gives a fuck? He's a Scouser.'
Liam 2000

. . .

On Paul Weller

'People think he's some deep god, but he's a moany old bastard. He's Victor Meldrew with a suntan.'
Noel 1995

. . .

Not that they always get it right, Noel gave this assessment of Jay-Z's planned headline slot at Glastonbury 2008

'If it ain't broke don't fix it. If you start to break it then people aren't going to go. I'm sorry, but Jay-Z? No chance. Glastonbury has a tradition of guitar music and even when they throw the odd curve ball in on a Sunday night you go "Kylie Minogue?" I don't know about it. But I'm not having hip-hop at Glastonbury. It's wrong.'
Noel 2008

. . .

In the event, the rapper used Noel's words for his intro tape and began his triumphant set by covering 'Wonderwall'. 'It was pretty funny,' Noel later conceded, though he got the last word, dissing Jay-Z's choice of guitar, declaring: 'I'm not sure one should be seen in public with a white Stratocaster.'

. . .

And then there's Blur. Despite initially appearing to get on when both bands first came face to face in 1994, a feud between Blur and Oasis quickly developed, leading to the ultimate Britpop showdown in 1995, when both bands squared up, releasing singles into the chart in the same week. Blur claimed Number One with 'Country House' over Oasis's 'Roll With It'. However, that was a mere skirmish in a war that fans of each side have since claimed their boys won: the Gallaghers going on to front the bigger band, staging some of the biggest gigs the planet has ever played host to, while Blur's Damon Albarn has become one of the most innovative artists of the age, forming the bands Gorillaz, The Good, The Bad and The Queen and writing operas.

. . .

'People from my band have been quoted as saying that they hate Blur but I'll say that although I've never been into a Blur album, I'll buy the singles compilation when it comes out. They're a great singles band, simple as that. Regardless of whether they hate us or we hate them.'
Noel 1994

. . .

Reacting to Blur picking up four Brit awards including Best Band and Best Album in February 1995

'Blur are a great pop band. 'Girls And Boys' was a good pop song, you know? But they're not as good as us. Last year they were Band of the Year, but it should have been us. All our singles charted, we had sell-out tours, we were top of the album charts. We should have been Band of the Year.'
Liam 1995

. . .

'Damon Albarn is a fucking knobber. And his guitarist – who I thought was all right – seems to think that he's some intelligent superhuman being, the fucking idiot. I never met the drummer and the bassist, who I first didn't like and thought he was a cunt, turned out to be quite all right. But I don't like the music, and I don't like the singer.'

Noel 1997

. . .

'I worked on building sites; that fundamentally makes my soul purer than theirs.'

Noel 2002

. . .

Responding to rumours that he and Blur's Alex James had become friends

'He's alright, he's one of those Hooray Henry boys. Hit him a slap every now and then and tell him to go to the bar. I wouldn't say he gets on well with us though. The only thing he gets on well with is his yacht.'

Liam 2000

. . .

On that chart showdown

'We had no problem with them until the
point when they started moving singles back
and forward.'
Noel 2002

.   .   .

Responding to Damon's influences
for 'Parklife'

'Why didn't he get into politics then if he was
dissatisfied by the shopping mall culture over
here? It just shows what a pompous arse he is. If
you've got time to worry about American society
creeping in over here, then I would get a proper
fucking job.'
Noel 2002

.   .   .

'That cunt is like "Is there a
bandwagon passing? Park it
outside my house." He'll be in a
heavy metal band next year
when it's fashionable.'

Noel 2002

.   .   .

mad for it

'The Blur/Oasis thing was very silly but it was fun. I meant every world I said. They're still a bunch of goons.'
Liam 2002

.   .   .

'You know Damon, bless him, I've got a lot of respect for him, I really mean it … Because I'm indifferent to Damon he thinks that I think he's a cunt. Our Liam will talk to him. I won't because he's just another singer in a band to me, but I don't think he's a cunt.'
Noel 2007

.   .   .

Following Blur's return after a near ten-year break in 2009

'[Blur] are in it for the money, aren't they, the fuckers? You won't catch Oasis reforming, y'know. Never.'
Liam 2010

.   .   .

You may have the impression that the Gallaghers hate all musicians, not so ...

'Listen, it's Charlotte Church for me, man. She could be the next Liam. She's got a great voice and she fucking has it. She knows how to get hammered and she freaks people out.'
Liam 2005

The Gallaghers
on Beliefs

Some bands have a habit of adopting some very questionable beliefs, from strange ancient sects who place their faith in cotton thread to new-fangled alien cults, musicians seem to possess a rare ability to not only believe the unbelievable, but also take it upon themselves to lecture the world about some very weird stuff as well. Fortunately, that was never going to be an issue for Noel or Liam. Hardened in Burnage in their youth, the Gallaghers have their own philosophy on pretty much everything. Just don't expect to like it …

. . .

On faith, life and death

'Our kid tends to take everything fucking literally.
He's a bit of a cosmic guy, a bit up in the sky.
He believes in spirituality and all that. I believe in
black 'n' white.'
Noel 1994

. . .

'Football is more important to
me than religion. Some pop
stars I like are more important
to me than God, so yeah, I
would hope we mean more to
people than putting money in a
church basket and saying ten
Hail Marys on Sunday. Has God
played Knebworth recently?'
Noel 1997

. . .

'Am I scared of dying? No because I've already
done it a couple of times and it's a piece of piss.
There's nothing to it, you just sit there and wait for
it to happen. Big deal.'
Liam 2000

. . .

On their funerals

'I'm not really bothered 'cause
I won't be there. I don't give
a shit.'
Noel 1998

. . .

'On my grave, I want them to write, "Don't fucking
come here with your bunches of flowers"'. I don't
want a gravestone, I want a V-sign, two fingers.
When you're dead, you're dead. It's now that
matters.'
Liam 1995

. . .

'We're all heathens. A few of us practise a faith but we're after something. I'm after something. I'll say no more than that in case I start to sound like Thom Yorke.'

Noel 2002

. . .

On excess

'Beer is the best drug ever!'
Liam 1994

. . .

'I'd been up for two days previous and I always had this mad theory that if anyone could break the 72-hour barrier they'd never need to sleep again. And, of course, that's not true because I ended up in fucking hospital.'

Noel 1995

. . .

'We do take too many drugs, though, and I wish I'd never started. In fact, I wish I'd never started smoking cigarettes or drinking beer or taking cocaine or ecstasy because I'd have a lot more money. The thing about us is we're honest. If we're asked whether we take drugs, we say yes. I was brought up by my mum not to be a liar.'
Noel 1996

. . .

'When I drink I don't fucking pussy about. I get stuck in there and get wasted and wake up the next day and think "fucking hell" then I leave off for a bit. I'm happy with my drinking situation.'
Liam 2001

. . .

'There's people in the Houses of Parliament, man, who are bigger heroin addicts and cocaine addicts than anyone in this room now. And it's all about honesty at the end of the day … Drugs is like getting up and having a cup of tea in the morning.'
Noel 1997

. . .

On being described as androgynous

'What does that mean? Explain. I'm a pretty boy, yeah. I'm a bit obsessed with my hair. You've got to have a decent haircut if you're the frontman of a band.'

Liam 2002

. . .

Always a snappy dresser, Liam now has his own label, Pretty Green

'I wouldn't say I was into fashion … just things that look good.'

Liam 2010

. . .

On sex

'Birds are all right. They're all pink on the inside.
Any bird who's fit is all right, unless she's nicked or
ugly and she speaks back to you. If she thinks I'm
boss, then thumbs up. Chicks in Japan don't even
ask your name, just, "Can I sleep with you
tonight?" "Certainly, my dear." I like American birds
till they open their mouths. Then they annoy me,
but if they're fit, they're fit.'
Liam 1996

. . .

'I'm not a fucking baby machine, though we're
[Liam and Nicole] mega at it.'
Liam 2002

. . .

On fame

'Who wants to be anonymous
anyway? I was anonymous
for 24 years ...'
Noel 1997

. . .

'Famous or not famous, I don't give a shit. Some famous people can be complete wankers.'
Liam 1997

. . .

'I go to more gigs than all the A&R men in Creation put together. [Fame] doesn't stop me going out, otherwise I'd just become a hermit sitting in my house all day wondering who's at the door. You can't live like that. If Mark Chapman is walking up the street, he's walking up the street. There's fuck all you can do about it.'
Noel 1997

. . .

And extraterrestrials ...

'Do I believe in aliens? Course I do. I'm not
frightened by them, though, I'm as smart as them.
Probably thick as fuck, aren't they? ... I'd do they
heads in, me, frighten the life out of them! That's
why they haven't landed yet.'

Liam 1997

Noel vs Liam

In the late hours of 28 August, 2009, Oasis officially split up. Deciding he could take no more, Noel walked away from the band following a dressing-room scrap at a festival in Paris that culminated in each of the Gallaghers smashing up treasured guitars belonging to the other. However, as is apparent from reading the brothers' opinions of each other, what was most surprising about the ending of Oasis was that they had lasted so long – though with quitting band members, Gallagher walk-outs and a massive punch-up in 2000, the group had had plenty of dress rehearsals for the break-up. Still, there's nothing like the real thing …

. . .

Never say never

'We'll never break up. We'll just call it a day, shake hands, say, "That was nice, don't you owe me a royalty cheque?" And that'll be it. We'll go down the pub and say, "That was great!" and get on with the next thing.'
Liam 1997

. . .

'If you'd asked around 3 December 1997 whether I thought Oasis would be around to celebrate their tenth birthday, I'd have laughed ever so politely in your face and said, "No fucking way!"'
Noel 2001

. . .

Following the 2000 punch-up, Noel stopped touring with the band briefly ...

'I lost it with him. It was a proper fight – it wasn't like, "I'll scratch your eyes out, you bitch!" It was a proper brawl and I'm actually quite proud of the fact that it came to blows. He knows if he crosses me that far I'll leave him in the shit.'
Noel 2000

. . .

Reflecting on that 2000 fight

'The fat lady hasn't started singing yet but she was definitely clearing her throat, having her lemon and honey, doing her scales. But she's not started the performance.'
Noel 2002

. . .

mad for it

However, by 2009 the fat lady was warming up again. By then the brothers were only communicating via blogs and Twitter, despite touring together

'We had a fucking ding-dong in the airport and I think he started crying then – that was it – doesn't travel with me any more ... so I never really see him, the only time I see him is onstage and we're a little bit busy at that time to be scratching each other.'
Liam 2009

. . .

In the build-up to their final split, Oasis played a rare intimate show at Camden's Roundhouse, which saw the brothers making verbal sideswipes at each other onstage, which they then followed up online.

. . .

Blogging after their last headline show at the Roundhouse

'What's'izname [Liam] exploded with pretend rage the minute he walked on. Strange cat. Probably on his man period. Saying that, it was a full moon 'n' all. Didn't notice him getting any more hairy though. Mind you, those that were there seemed to enjoy it, so … y'know, onwards and sideways.'
Noel 2009

. . .

Which triggered this reply via Twitter

'Regarding short arse's comments on my behaviour at the Roundhouse, pretend rage? It's called rock 'n' roll darling you wanna try it sometime! Man period? You've been on since the first gig [of the tour] in Seattle!'
Liam 2009

. . .

A couple of weeks later, and following that Paris gig, Noel issued a statement in which he declared he had 'no other option than to get me cape and seek pastures new'

'The last 18 years have been truly, truly amazing (and I hate that word, but today is the one time I'll deem it appropriate). A dream come true. I take with me glorious memories.'
Noel 2009

. . .

Not that the Oasis split has settled anything between the Gallaghers ...

'Oasis ran its course ... He wanted to chill a bit – our kid's not rock 'n' roll. I am. I'm still going for it till the day I die.'
Liam 2010

. . .

Responding to a fan at a 2010 solo gig

'For the record that guy said, "Where's Liam?". He's probably being a real northerner somewhere designing the perfect desert boot.'
Noel 2010

. . .

Still, if the fat lady has a tune left in her, an opera based on the Gallaghers' trials and tribulations has been suggested …

'I don't think two blokes having the same fucking argument for sixteen years over and over is the stuff of opera. *Oasis: The Opera* would be very short.'
Noel 2009

. . .

Don't worry, Oasis may be gone but you'll be seeing plenty more of the Gallaghers in the years to come, Noel has solo plans while Liam has already formed a new band called Beady Eye

'Beady Eye is proper rock 'n' roll. Oasis was a pop band compared to what we're doing.'
Liam 2010

. . .

mad for it

Not that Noel is in a hurry to get his solo career up and running

'll see you somewhere down the road ... Now, if you'll excuse me I have a family and a football team to indulge.'
Noel 2009

. . .

And for those who think the split is just a way to stage a reunion, think again ...

'The only reason why Oasis will come back is when we're fucking skint. I'm far from skint as you can tell - and I won't be skint for a long, long fucking time.'
Liam 2010

Afterwords

mad for it

And finally, the Gallaghers' mini 'master plan' for the perfect life

'I'm mad for it … I'm a lad and that's fucking that.'
Liam 1995

. . .

'I put a lot of faith in people's ears.'
Noel 1995

. . .

'I fucking hate sleeping, me. Boring! I wish I didn't have to sleep, it's such a waste of time. I'd rather be up, living.'
Liam 1997

. . .

'I don't think I'm ordinary because I'm not. I'm special because I'm very, very talented.'
Noel 2003

. . .

'I've got a bit of [John] Lennon and now a bit of [Muhammad] Ali. I've got two loudmouth arrogant bastards living inside me.'
Liam 1997

. . .

'I never said I was wrong. I'm just saying I wasn't right at that particular time.'
Noel 1998

. . .

'You can be cool with kids and you can still be cool when you're fucking 50.'
Liam 2001

. . .

'You pay peanuts, you get monkeys on crack.'
Liam 2009

mad for it